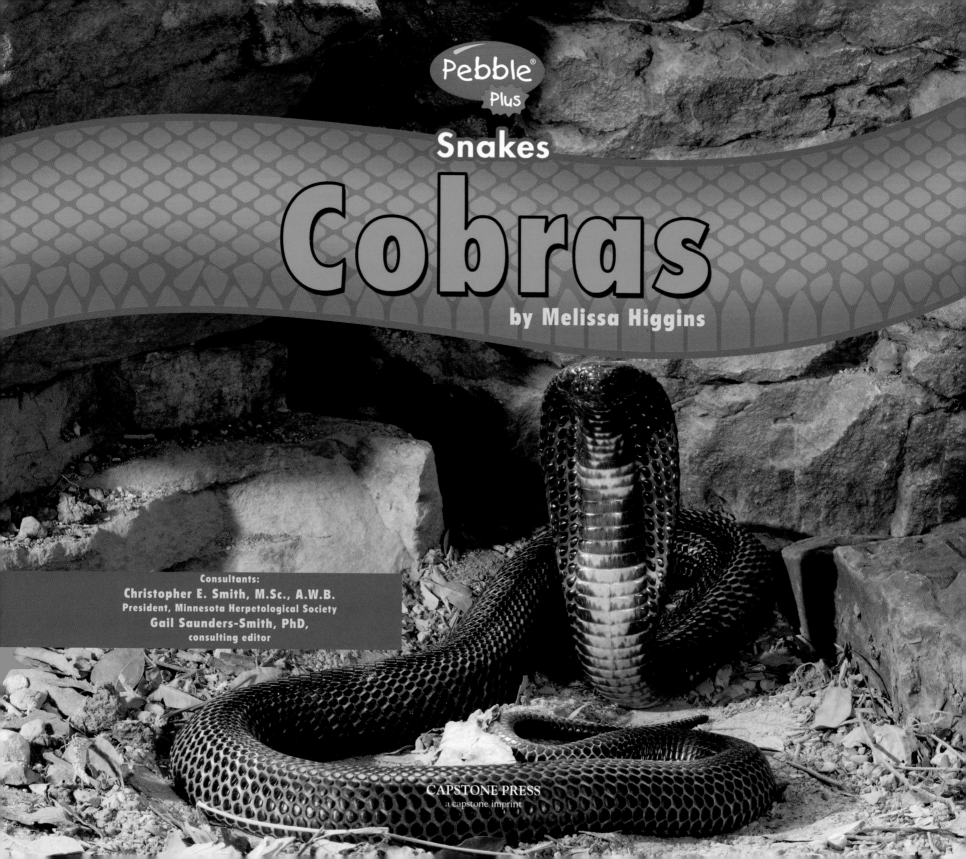

Pebble® Plus

Snakes

Cobras

by Melissa Higgins

Consultants:
Christopher E. Smith, M.Sc., A.W.B.
President, Minnesota Herpetological Society

Gail Saunders-Smith, PhD,
consulting editor

CAPSTONE PRESS
a capstone imprint

Pebble Plus is published by Capstone Press,
1710 Roe Crest Drive, North Mankato, Minnesota 56003.
www.capstonepub.com

Library of Congress Cataloging-in-Publication Data
Higgins, Melissa, 1953–
Cobras / by Melissa Higgins.
p. cm.—(Pebble plus. Snakes)
Summary: "Simple text and full-color photographs describe cobras"—Provided by publisher.
Audience: 005-008.
Audience: K to grade 3.
Includes bibliographical references and index.
ISBN 978-1-4765-2070-4 (library binding)
ISBN 978-1-4765-3483-1 (eBook PDF)
1. Cobras—Juvenile literature. I. Title.
QL666.O64H54 2013
597.96'42—dc23   2013007427

Editorial Credits
Jeni Wittrock, editor; Kyle Grenz, designer; Eric Manske, production specialist

Photo Credits
Alamy: AfriPics.com, 5, Biju, 21, Mark Boulton, 9, PhotoShot Holdings Ltd, 7; Corbis: George Logan, 15, Visuals Unlimited/Jim Merli, 19; Dreamstime: Dennis Donohue, 1, Neil Harrison, 17; Shutterstock: Heiko Kiera, 11, Nicolaas Weber, cover, vlastas66, design element (throughout); SuperStock: NHPA, 13

Note to Parents and Teachers

The Snakes set supports national science standards related to biology and life science. This book describes and illustrates cobras. The images support early readers in understanding the text. The repetition of words and phrases helps early readers learn new words. This book also introduces early readers to subject-specific vocabulary words, which are defined in the Glossary section. Early readers may need assistance to read some words and to use the Table of Contents, Glossary, Read More, Internet Sites, and Index sections of the book.

Printed in the United States of America in North Mankato, Minnesota.
092015   009189R

Table of Contents

Warning!

A 6-foot- (1.8-meter-) long cobra tastes the air with its flicking tongue. Danger! The cobra tastes its enemy, a mongoose.

The cobra rises up.

It puffs out its hood.

The cobra is warning the

mongoose to stay away.

Africa and Asia

There are more than 20 kinds of cobras. These reptiles live in the grasslands, deserts, and forests of Africa and Asia.

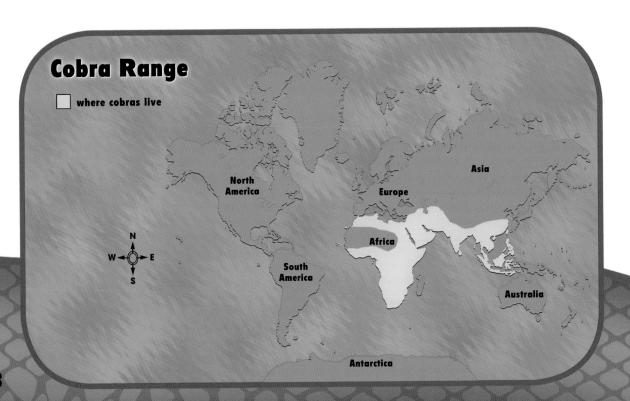

Cobra Range

☐ where cobras live

North America

Europe

Asia

Africa

South America

Australia

Antarctica

N
W E
S

Cobras lie in morning sun, warming their cold blood. If the day gets hot, cobras rest in the shade.

Super Venom

At sunset a cobra begins to hunt. It searches for rats, rabbits, and toads. Cobras even eat other snakes.

Strike! The cobra sinks
sharp fangs into its prey.
Venom shoots through
holes in the fangs.

Venom stops the prey's breathing and heartbeat. A big meal can last the cobra a month or more.

Cobra Life

Female cobras lay between 12 and 60 eggs at a time. Most cobras guard their eggs until they hatch.

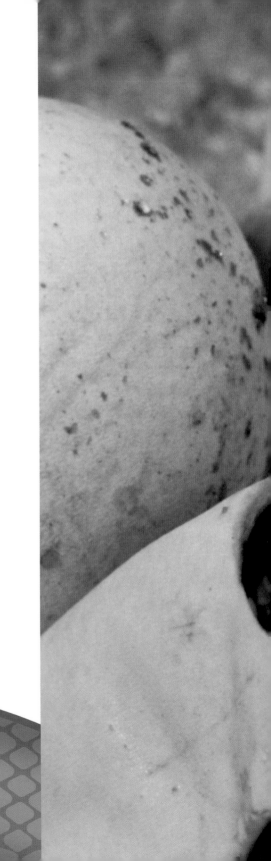

Baby cobras can open their hoods as soon as they hatch. Cobras live 20 years or more in the wild.

Glossary

fang—a clawlike tooth; cobras' fangs squirt out venom

grassland—large area of wild grasses

hood—part of a cobra's neck; a cobra creates its hood by sticking out its ribs

mongoose—a mammal with a long body and striped fur that lives in Africa and Asia

prey—an animal hunted by another animal for food

reptile—a cold-blooded animal that breathes air and has a backbone; most reptiles have scales

venom—a liquid poison made by an animal to kill its prey

Read More

Gunderson, Megan M. *King Cobras.* Snakes. Edina, Minn.: ABDO Pub., 2011.

Sexton, Colleen. *Cobras.* Snakes Alive. Minneapolis: Bellwether Media, 2010.

White, Nancy. *King Cobras: The Biggest Venomous Snakes of All!* Fangs. New York: Bearport Pub., 2009.

Internet Sites

FactHound offers a safe, fun way to find Internet sites related to this book. All of the sites on FactHound have been researched by our staff.

Here's all you do:

Visit *www.facthound.com*

Type in this code: 9781476520704

Check out projects, games and lots more at
www.capstonekids.com

Index

Word Count: 170
Grade: 1
Early-Intervention Level: 16